Under A Riverbed Sky

By

Christopher Woods

Panther Creek Press

Spring, Texas

Published by Panther Creek Press
116 Tree Crest Circle
P.O. Box 130233
Panther Creek Station
Spring, TX 77393-0233

Cover photograph by Linda Woods
Cover design by Pamela Copus,
Sonic Media, Inc., Plano, Texas

Manufactured in the United States of America
Printed and bound by Data Duplicators, Inc., Houston, Texas

1 2 3 4 5 6 7 8 9 10

Library of Congress Cataloguing in Publication Data

Woods, Christopher
    Under a riverbed sky

    I. Title   II. Prose   III. Poetry

ISBN 0-9678343-4-1

Acknowledgments

All of these pieces have appeared previously in journals or anthologies, sometimes in different forms. To the editors of these publications, all acknowledgments and appreciation are due.

Air Fish, The Albany Review, Arrowsmith, Asylum, Aura Literary/ Arts Review, Austin Writer, Blue Light Red Light, Blue Mesa Review, Bohemian Chronicles, The Brobdingnagian Times, Chaminade Literary Review, Chiricu, City Scriptum, Columbia, The Fractal, Foliage, Foolscap, Global Tapestry Journal, Gopherwood Review, Grow Old Along With Me, Gypsy, Gypsy Blood Review, Happy, Idiom 23, Labrys, The Ledge, Liquid Ohio, The Lowell Pearl, Maelstrom The Maverick Press, Mind Matters Review, New England Review, New Kauri, Newsletter Inago, Next Phase, Nexus, Novoy, Oasis, Pangolin Papers, Passager, Piddiddle, The Plaza, Poetry Forum, Portland Magazine, Printed Matter, The Prose Poem, Protea, Quarry, Red Dance Floor, Riverrun, Roanoke Review, The Saturday Museum, Seems, Sepia, Short Story International, Shockbox, Simple Vows, Sivullen, The Sunflower Collection, Suddenly, Takahe, Touchstone, The Ucross Anthology, Una Mas Magazine, The Urbanite, Waves, The Wildflower Collection, Writer's Forum, Xavier Review.

"Wants" appeared, *in different form, as a limited edition broadside from West Rose Press*

"The Sea Changes" appears in Writing on Water, *edited by David Rothenberg and Marta Ulvaeus (a Terra Nova book, MIT Press)*

Some of the pieces in this collection were written during a residency at THE UCROSS FOUNDATION in Wyoming. The author wishes to thank THE UCROSS FOUNDATION for their generosity, and for the serenity they provide artists of all kinds.

Contents

Contents, *continued:*

Christopher Woods

for Linda

FOREST

It has a way of changing, the tree you found years ago now. While walking, or driving, or in a book. Perhaps a tree you dreamed. And no matter what has happened since, that tree remains.

But it is always different. Sometimes you remember it alone on a hillside. Other times, it blends with others like old, cloistered nuns.

It has a gift for coming and going without stirring the roots below. In fact, if I were to tell you this again next year, we too will have changed. Turned up dirt, cast our limbs about, but never able to break completely free from ourselves.

In a forest, in a room, something never rests.

BEASTS

They have no need to speak of milestones passed. Or gloat where air is sour, full of smoke and the breath of champagne.

Unlikely they will migrate from old haunts to new *cul de sacs* in bland new towns where trees have never grown.

No use for shimmering rocks strung on string around their necks. Or the zigzagging car, humming with computer wit.

Their victory is unheralded in silent fields alive with night. It rustles in leaves, wind and utterly blind faith. Song of things decomposing, then beginning again.

Song they have no need of singing.

THE WOODS: FOUR VISITATIONS

One

The path approached, passed beneath them, then fell behind. They moved slowly, she supporting him. On this winter night it came to her that, in so many layers of clothing, she could not feel his body heat. Only hers. She pulled him closer. In earnest.

"That hurts," he said.

"I'm sorry, but you don't need another fall."

When he sighed, she watched smoke flare from his nostrils to either side of his head. He was a frail dragon, walking in tame woods. Time had killed what was primitive in the woods. Now, in their old age, she realized that the woods were probably much more civilized than they were.

His hair was thin, white, windblown tufts. Better off than he was, she knew she would survive him, would have to bury him after watching him die.

Would there be someone to do the same for her? On any walk, she knew, there was always someone ahead or behind.

"Let's turn back now," he said.

"Only a little more. We'll catch the other trail and follow it home."

Now too cold to argue, he grabbed her hand and held it as an owl flew over their heads. It vanished into the night gloom of trees. They kept walking.

"There it is," she announced, seeing the other trail.

"I'm happy for it," he said, his voice chilly as the night.

In their house they had left a fire burning.

Two

They did not fear the night. Not silent slugs oozing with directive across autumn leaves. Or the crackling forest floor, ground so brittle that even the footsteps of ghosts resounded endlessly.

In a bag she carried insect repellent, a bottle of red Bordeaux and two kinds of cheese. He carried the old plaid blanket slung over his shoulder.

This was a night of celebration. They had feigned illness and skipped cocktails at a neighbor's home. Here were the trails they themselves had made, one weekend after the next, for years. Here, they could walk blindfolded.

"My insomnia might go away outdoors," he said.

"Maybe we won't want to sleep," she said hopefully, and she surprised even herself.

They left the trail and went crashing into underbrush, finally coming to a small clearing where a fountain bubbled and whispered. The wine and cheese finished, they watched the sky through firs that framed their field of vision.

"You know I'm sorry about that," he said at last.

After all, he had strayed from the path only recently. The night sky of many distances made him consider this.

"It's over," she said. "Isn't all that over?"

He cupped her chin with his hand until his lips took over. She didn't resist. After some weeks of his constant absence, she had taken him back, preferring not to start life over again alone.

Much later in the night, both of them covered with dew and the air thick with fog, he got up. He was going back to the house for another blanket. Moving about in the dark, he wished aloud for a flashlight.

"I'll go with you," she said. "A person could get lost."

Three

"And why not?" he asked angrily. He was infuriated that she would refuse him.

"It's not time," she said. "Not yet." Defensive about denying him, she also feared his wrath.

On the new plaid blanket, on a night in a high school year, their clothes in a pile on summer grass, their sweat glistened until they smelled like the same person.

He got up, standing with a foot on either side of her waist. His eyes brimmed with rage. He was aroused, the same as she. Then, in a quick movement he turned and walked away, disappearing into the trees. Not bothering to cover herself, she followed.

She wanted him, no doubt of that. But she feared that, by giving in, she might be giving him away. After savoring the moment, he might begin looking for different moments.

She found him kneeling in a gully, spilling himself in a small stream. She wanted to go to him, pull him down in the stream and please him, but before she moved an inch he had begun moaning like a pained animal in a trap. Afterwards, she watched him clean himself with eucalyptus leaves.

Four

Ignoring warnings of a one-eyed troll, furry and brandishing fingernails the length of Spanish daggers, they entered the woods. The bright spring morning dissipated in the hushed dank air beneath the trees. Poison berries weighed down limbs over the path.

"We could get lost," she said, six years old and fearful of most things.

"Follow me and we won't," he said. He was a year older.

They found no troll. Instead, they discovered the place where bums slept at night. Excavating the hobo inner sanctum, they scattered the ashes from old fires.

By afternoon they were lost, by nightfall certain they would never be found alive. Their cries were heard only by melancholy owls. Very late, there were voices from a search party. Flashlights appeared, coming and going like the small migrations of fireflies. The closer the lights came, the more the vines hanging from trees became the corpses of snakes, limp and bloodless.

And despite lectures received once safe at home again, they knew they would enter the woods again.

SAYING IT

Tell me, she'd say. I wasted no time. I spit it out, like it was a natural thing. Maybe it was. But strange, too. I'd a vague sensation of having said it before. To her? Well, if not, then to someone else. Probably to many.

Miraculously, for a moment, everything was good again. She seemed pleased that I'd say it, just the way she wanted to hear it.

Say it again, she'd say. Oh boy, I thought. But I'd do it. Say it. Hope it would be right. Could bring us a little shard of happiness.

Which is how I'd like it to be, all said. Why I'm here now, in fact. Like this, watching for her. If she comes, she'll ask. Like I've always imagined. I'll say it, then. Be done with it.

For now, though, I'm still waiting, hoping she'll be here. Praying I remember the words. They're on the tip of my tongue. They're ready to fly...

IF I SEE HER AGAIN

If I see her again I will tell her this and that, a little of both perhaps. But the truth is that I know she won't be coming back. Not tomorrow, not for a thousand tomorrows standing side by side on a wall that disappears beyond the hills.

Maybe, later, I will know how all this happens, how you can reach out and there is nothing, no one, reaching back.

If that happens, she will explain not with words but with a smile. She'll begin moving around this very room. She'll be stirring inside somehow. Begin dancing, just as she always did.

I look a thousand nights ahead and remember as many days back, but there is no seeing her, not now or then or in the time in between.

Until I see her again I'll be content to imagine her. The way she came and went away, the way she never was...

TALISMAN

Maybe I find it along a road. Abandoned, with a skin of dust. I bend down to get a better look. Wonder how long it's been there, if time and the elements have brittled it. The desire to touch it is intense. Nothing else, I imagine, will feel quite the same way this does.

Quickly, then, like a thief, I grab hold of it. Discover it is still warm. Still feeling someone else's touch. Puzzling, how such a thing could be let go, surrendered, of no importance to anyone. Forsaken on a road in harsh sunlight.

That night, or one soon after, I decide to go to work. I make use of it. I handle it like I know how, as if this were some knowledge I already possessed.

And I discover something. The thing itself is leading me on. Page after page, is what I mean. On a poet's road. Through the night, into the dawn. Thought after darting thought.

Not questioning, I follow. I work like any deaf star, aware of falling but not the sound of the descent. Or even the reason for it. I labor with an odd kind of fever. But I finish a poem, and then another. Night after night after finding this thing along the road.

Before or after this, I can't be sure, something else comes to mind. That these poems must belong not to me but to someone else. Poems that, by accident or worse, someone else was unable to write. It bothers me, this strange kind of borrowing. But for the moment, before or after, I do nothing about it.

Then, one morning this way or that, I find myself walking. Out on that same road again. I stop in the very same place where I discovered it. I lay the thing down in the dust, just as I had come across it. I take care to wipe away any scents or markings I imagine I have left on it. But I have been careful, even respectful, I know. No harm is done.

Before I turn to go, I say some small, random things. Not a prayer, you understand, but silent words with the same curious zeal. I stand up to go. I turn away. I leave it there, along that road in the harsh sunlight. I don't look back.

Whoever comes along next will want it this way, I know. To discover it for themselves, just as I did. Dust clinging to it. The overall sensation of this thing being left, handed down. To them. It will be their blessing then. Their problem.

No reason why this shouldn't continue. On and on, until the true owner comes to reclaim the thing. I imagine this sometimes. How he will hold it to his ear. How she will listen for the sounds of all the places it has been. How they will know us all by our smell.

By then it will no longer be my concern, where it goes, with whom, for how long or short a time. All I know, all I have to go on, is how I felt when I put it down in the dust. Dead and still warm at the same time. Walking away from it, the film of it all, I mean. Sun blazing, dust clouds blinding my every step.

THE WELL

Forget, for the moment, the women who gather there talking, waiting to fill pitchers. And forget for now the dirty faced children who twist their mothers' skirts, who spit at one another, and who toss laughter like small clouds into the air. Forget all that.

What matters now is this one man, bent and nameless, who has slowed there, so close to the well. For him, now, even walking has become a curse. What he thinks about as he walks is the agony that, until now, he has tried to resist. Breathing deeply, he swallows one child's laugh, then another.

Slowly he circles the well, feels it pulling him into its bosom. Nearby, sitting on benches, are other old men. Maybe they have been there forever. He remembers running past them when he was still a child.

He never had time to stop, to talk to them. Or as a man in middle age, passing but not really seeing them. And later, his own hair and beard white, he had looked away rather than think about them. He would have no part of all that.

Until now. He circles until he finds a place to sit. He is lucky. The bench is still warm from someone else. He wonders whose place he has taken, and where they have gone. For a few minutes? Forever? And he wonders how long he will remain there, within the pull of the well, the lure of its depth. All that.

Maybe, he thinks, it won't be so bad. Feeding on the circular darkness that grows out of the earth. Watching children passing. The older men who look away. Even the tired old men who stand so near to the well, all of them waiting patiently for a seat.

HIS CITY

Coming up the road in that sad region, he thought he recognized a tree. First one, then another. Finally, he recognized an entire line of trees. Suddenly, he remembered having helped plant them, many years before. It came to him that he had been away a long time, perhaps thirty years if the trees could be trusted. They were mere saplings when he left.

Doubtless this city, Bastillo, had changed greatly in that amount of time. Other men his age had married, had fathered children. His former friends had worked alongside each other in this city, the one he never believed was his own. He had banished himself from it. The only things he had touched, it seemed, were the trees, and now they didn't recognize him. He was thinking about this, how nothing seemed to belong to him, when he came into the city.

Maybe some of his friends were already dead, he didn't know. Maybe buried outside the city in the ground he had always thought too dusty. His city would be sturdy. Built on more rocky terrain. His city, he was sure, would not rise from a dusty plain in such a sad region. Not his city.

No one he passed in the streets paid him much mind. Certainly no one recognized him. He realized he too would have a hard time recognizing someone he used to know. After all, he was more familiar with the faces of people in his own city, wasn't he? Could he really be expected to remember all these faces, and from so long ago? Then too, a fact remained. The people in this city were the stuff of someone else's dream.

So it came as something of a surprise when a woman he passed in the square stopped and stared at him. After a moment, she began weeping and put her arms around him. An old woman, eightyish, she was dressed in yellow muslin, her eyes as sad as the land itself.

Gently, careful not to frighten the old woman, he pushed her to the side to be free of her. If it was still there, he was thinking, there was a house he needed to see. He set out for the street that led to that house. But there were so many new streets now, maybe a hundred more than he remembered, and soon he felt as though he was merely wandering.

Even if the old woman had begun following him now, even if she was crying so mournfully, he would not stop. He would not slow his gait, or even turn to look at her again. He ignored her cries, and would not admit that he was her son. All that was someone else's dream, being born here, he knew. It was a brittle kind of knowledge that, if left to fester, would only confuse him. He began walking faster, leaving the old woman behind him.

He did not find the house he wished to see that first afternoon. There was not time enough before the sun went down. Some things had not changed. No electricity in the city, just as he remembered. His city would have electricity. It would have running water. His city would never be without ample food and drink. His city would not be in such a sad region.

When darkness fell, when he finally stopped walking, when the weeping old woman was only another soiled memory, he stood on the bank of a river. He could feel the breeze off the water and smell the muddy shore, but the darkness hid the river itself. He could smell food being cooked somewhere nearby, down the darkness of the bank. And he could hear voices.

They took him in, a small band of workers who would sleep on a bluff above the unseen water flow. If they recognized him, they didn't let on. With them in the darkness, listening to their talk, he realized they were young enough to be his sons. They didn't ask him where he was coming from, or where he was going.

He asked them for a bit of work, he didn't care what, and that made them accept him. They gave him some food, and a blanket. Maybe he'd be one of their own kind, that's all they could have thought.

He had decided, early on, that in his city there would be no such thing as hard work. It could only mean that all the people who had come before, who had toiled the long centuries through, had worked in vain. They hadn't been able to get rid of it, of work. All they did was work toward something, but no one seemed to know what it was. It just kept going on. Going on.

Of course he didn't tell the others about his city, and the fact of little work. Such information might make them edgy, and perhaps suspicious. And he didn't complain about how exhausted he was by the following afternoon, when the cargo loading was done.

What kind of work was it? They had loaded a small steamship with what appeared to be some kind of native product packed in large wooden crates. He didn't know what it was he had struggled with all day. All he knew was that the cargo smelled half of tar and half of dust, and that it was going somewhere else.

When work was finished, the men scurried to their places on the bluff again. He walked slowly, allowing them to get ahead of him. By the time they reached the bluff, he was nowhere to be seen, by any of them.

There was still that house he wanted to see. The Bastillo house, it was called. A famous house. Bastillo had been the first man to come along and make a camp on the dusty plain near the river. He brought others along with him. Still others, passing through the sad region and feeling forlorn, also arrived and stayed. A city came from nothing but dust and blood and the river, and Bastillo named it all after himself.

It was Bastillo's house he looked for, street after street, in the final daylight. After dark, he felt his way, house by house.

An hour passed, then another. He spoke to no one, as there was no one in the streets. He knew they were already sleeping, passing time until the work business started up again. Started up again.

He was lucky, for even in the darkness, he saw the gables of the Bastillo house. The roof was so steep that it appeared to pierce the sky. A house like this is not so hard to remember, he thought. It was exactly as he remembered it, in fact, as he had hated it for some long years now.

He unlatched the front gate and walked directly below the great veranda of the house. The stairs did not moan as his weight shifted from one step to the next. Then, standing before the front door, he thought about all the time he had been away, and about how far he had walked. And how much hate had played a part. How it was hate which had propelled him to return.

He could no longer contain his anger. He spat on the door and the beveled windows. He spat on the wicker chairs and tables that graced the wide veranda. Finally, when his mouth was dry, he retraced his steps back down the stairs and to the gate. He went back like he had come, street after street, until he was once again at the edge of the city. The farther from the city he walked, the more he could feel the heavy sadness of the plain lifting. In his mind, the air seemed to clear.

In time, it would clear enough for him to know the place for his own city when he came to it. Bastillo had been found during a flood. Bastillo's small boat had capsized in the river, and he swam ashore before anyone else. A high river tide had given him a city to call his own.

So he felt that his own city was something he could be certain about, nearer or farther on that road. Or in a storm. Or sometimes as they come, in a dream. He believed that his city would come in the latter fashion. So he slept much, and dreamed. In his city, with no work to steal his time, he could sleep and dream as much as he pleased.

21

But his sleep was anxious. He was in a hurry for a voice to come to him and direct him to his city. He was getting older now. All those trips to other cities had aged him greatly. Sadly, his memory was dimming with age. It had become a problem, trying to recall which cities he had already visited, and which houses he had spat upon.

In the end, though, he had no choice. All he could do was to keep on.

Keep on.

THE DOOR

Nothing I can say you don't already know, or haven't passed through. If you have heard this, know this, don't let on. I need to hear a sound, the very noise of my voice.

And the noise of my thoughts. Tell you of winters so long and bitter that frosted trees gathered close to me, begging to come inside. The frozen blue breath of firs spoke of every sadness there is in this world, and maybe the next.

Listen, my hinges sing of lost, wandering words that still echo on the path outside. Hum grey, creaking tunes of things broken down, departed, disappeared.

But it is the haste of hands I remember best. Their touch, flinging my heart open wide. However time is, however it must be, I know the only lasting thing is silence. It does not leave, or even breathe.

It only rages, either side of me.

DETAIL FROM THE BLUE REPUBLIC

This room has blended into me, and I into it. This much is certain, but either the room remains unaware of my presence, or it is simply unconcerned. It broods, ever so silently, behind dust covered photographs. Behind canvases stretched across walls to hide the boundaries of this small expanse.

It is the wallpaper, the skin of this room, which most fascinates me. The paper is consistent throughout the room, a seemingly redundant Parisian street scene, circa 1900, involving a miniature cast.

A woman with a blue dress walks with a young child, a girl, at her side. The child is quite blue as well. They are making their way across a blue intersection which is otherwise empty. Emptiness, here, is rendered in splotches of blue, defined by linear charcoal strokes. There are no carriages, no horses, and this is still some time before the motor coach.

What *is* she carrying? Under her arm she holds something green, hazy and undefinable. And, even though I have often speculated on this mysterious package, I am still undecided. An enormous load of asparagus spears? Something she plans to exchange at the blue shop she approaches?

And while the woman and child remain there, frozen mid-step in mid-street, there is yet another woman in much the same state. Short and squat, and also blue from shoes to coiffure, she lingers at a jumbled newsstand. I imagine she is middle-aged, but it is mere speculation. Her back is to me. She is facing into the woodwork of this room, so I shall never know. This much is certain, though. She has yet to choose a magazine or newspaper. Instead, she leans on her right leg, composed and deliberate, as though consciously posing for a wallpaper scene.

To the left of the newsstand and a few steps up the street (steps the blue mother and child have yet to take), there is a tiny sidewalk café, done in the predictable, in blue. It is so small an establishment that one solitary table comprises its size. A lone, somewhat slender man occupies one of two chairs at that table, upon which nothing has been laid. Perhaps he waits for a companion, or for a lover. But I have an uncanny sense that he arrived alone for this eternal wait in the blue café.

But like the woman lingering at the newsstand, the man is also staring away, into the woodwork. Perhaps this is something they have in common, a need to escape recognition. Maybe their steps are heavy with guilt, as is often the case with accomplices.

Or, it might be very simply explained in another way. They look away because they share an abhorrence for the blue woman and child. They have tactfully delivered themselves from a possible confrontation by gazing into blue nothingness.

All of this, complex as it seems, is rendered in less than a square foot of space. It is repeated several hundred times around the room. Always it remains there, waiting for my return home.

They remain. The citizens of this blue republic are quite vigilant. And yet, something else need be said. They are not without a certain kind of tediousness.

Others who come to visit me here make no mention of these people. Curiously enough, though, some will remark on the omnipresent blue nature of my room. But they make no effort to trace it to the source, to Paris. Oh, I readily agree with them most of the time, it is very much a cold womb of a room. That will usually suffice. Yet I am obsessed with it. I feel a kind of trauma, a stifled empathy for these nameless people so near yet so far from one another. And of course their proximity to me. I matter here too, I tell them. But do they listen?

So I hang one more photograph to hide them, stretch one more canvas to reassure myself that I am not yet a citizen of the blue republic. So far, it has been enough. For now, it has held back the walls. For now.

TWO ROOMS

When she needed a smoke, she'd go outside, rainy or not. His orders. Her loose blouse willy-nilly with the wind, her tired black slacks layered unevenly with cat hair. He'd watch her in the yellow glow of the slab porch light, breathing. Always breathing. No matter she was sad, no matter she was left alone.

Except for him, her only son. Now, in the white months, it was very close in the two rooms. If their paths back and forth across chocolate shag could be traced, he knew their world would be revealed as a web. Strand by sticky strand, he could feel life coming up and around him, closing in, crushing his windpipe.

He too was alone, wasn't he? If only his old wife could see him now, she'd surely leave him all over again. The same two rooms had gotten smaller then, before, and it had gotten hard to breathe.

He didn't know what to make of it. Maybe it was the rooms, both of them, commanding fate. Maybe the rooms waited for the people to come, pair after pair, lost souls wandering the earth, coming home to roost. Then, once the people were settled in, the rooms made sure their world collapsed.

What else could make a man hate his mother so? He blamed their every quarrel on the rooms. When the final words were hurled, they both retreated to a room, like crossing a border into neutral land.

He'd sit in the dark, fists clenched at the sides of his head, trying to drown out the sound of her voice. She would be sitting, rocking back and forth, singing songs from the Fifties to shout down his from the Nineties.

Then, at some hour of the night he would get up and close the door between them. He'd leave her like that, sad asleep in front of the silent television, its glare continually changing, the room brighter, then darker. Electric breath.

And he would lie in bed with his face to the wall and wish for other things, oh, he wasn't sure what.

THE PAUSE

It came in the middle of talk. Something he had begun, or something she was finishing. Or perhaps they both spoke at once. But then the talk would stop. Completely. So quickly that the new silence was like a glimmer of sun balanced on a sea swell.

At that instant, the photo moment, for a shard of brief seconds there was nothing but this amazing silence in the air between them. The silence was a kind of abyss.

He noticed it, the same as she. How their words vanished, how whatever they were together lapsed, leaving them each alone. They were powerless to change it. All they could do was to wait for it to finish, for the pause to be over so that they might begin again.

EVERY HOUSE IS A WORLD

Now, after spending the better part of the day in bed, they sipped wine and read the afternoon newspaper. For a long time, they passed sections back and forth in silence. It was a consecrated hour, as hours go. It seemed that nothing else needed to be said. Finally, when the light had begun to fade in the window, he spread the paper out on his lap and cleared his throat.

"If I had to describe us," he said, "we would be like an old cathedral. Lasting, you know."

She considered this for a moment, and began to smile. She ran her green fingernails across his wide chest, then traced the small line of hair down his stomach.

"Us, a church?" she asked. This was a revelation to her.

They both began laughing, she because of his statement, he because she had tickled him in a tender place.

"A physical cathedral," he explained. "Nothing more."

He took her wandering hand and anchored it in his own. It amazed him still, how long and lovely her hands were. And how they fit so nicely inside his own. He ran his fingertip across her palm, tracing her lifeline. Then he placed his palm against hers. She then laced her fingers around his. Together, their fingers made steeples.

"We aren't as stone cold as that," she said. "Like a dark old church. Not us."

She ran her tongue over her lips and made them shiny again. No, they weren't like that at all, she was sure. They still had fires inside them. Wasn't the afternoon proof of that? Then she stopped and thought about it. Was he trying to tell her something? Some sad, or final?

He ran his finger across her still wet lips, and leaned over to kiss her. He could not remember ever having wanted someone this badly, or this often. When he saw the confused look in her soft, dark eyes, he realized he had not made himself clear.

"Don't you remember," he said, "the summer we visited all those cathedrals in France? How they had lasted? Supported from the outside?"

"Buttresses, you mean?"

He nodded. "Right. Sturdy stuff. Moored in the earth."

"I see now," she said, quite relieved.

"Good, then. That's how it is, this thing between us."

He put his arms around her and drew her body next to his. Her head resting on his chest, he played with the long strands of her dark hair. He pulled a strand through his mouth and bit it gently. He was certain, he had never felt like this before, with anyone. The rarity of it, the simple joy of her, was a thing he could not now imagine living without. In the past, he had not known anything like this. In the past, he decided, he had not even been alive.

"Someday," she said, making steeples again, "all cathedrals will be like this. Rising up to the sky."

"We don't need sky," he said gently. "Just earth. Sturdy, and solid. Something else might bring bad luck."

"You're probably right," she said. "Let's leave it the way it is."

Through the window, unknown to them, the moon was rising. A slight gust of wind blew across the bed. Without another word, he shifted his body, moving until she was beneath him. They began moving slowly then, deliberately, like all the hours on either side of them now.

WHAT HAPPENS

There were times in the night when he really believed she was nothing more than an interruption in his life, and he the same in hers.

They passed in the hall, each going a separate way. It wasn't a matter of good or bad as something that happened, in the present, in the past, who could know, it might always be that way.

But he also believed that time did not enter into this as much as space itself. Space between them, between most things, widened and narrowed, not for good or ill. Somehow it was all arranged, or else it arranged itself.

He didn't know which, of course, and he didn't know why. But the fact of the matter was that he was aware of this at night more than any other time.

THE NIGHT BLIND

Moving away from it now, our house of causes, lights like eyes that scour the darkness, I begin to disappear. If I hold out my hand far enough, it is lost entirely. Fall a step behind, I lose sight of you.

No moon glow finds the road or illuminates the pond with night wind on its cheek.

This is an experiment in the sanctuary of night. We know it can go both ways, or many.

We move away from each other, from every small cause that weds us. Slowly, then, the nights, the sequence, the last light going out.

HOME AGAIN, HOME AGAIN

I was not thinking about how far I had walked. When I finally did look up, it surprised me, how little distance I had actually covered. There was the yellow house with white trim that stood on posts behind the dune.

I did not know the people who lived in the yellow house. I did know that the husband was often drunk, and that he yelled at his wife just as often. I have heard it late at night as I walk this stretch of beach.

Some nights the screams are louder than the wind off the water. I never mention any of this to my wife. Somehow I believe she is better off without this kind of knowledge.

It amazed me to see the yellow house. I assumed that I had walked beyond the familiar things, houses and beach bars, lifeguard stands and abandoned sand castles, everything somehow essential, within reach. I laughed aloud, and knew no one could hear me. I laughed because, this time, like so many times before, I had succeeded in fooling myself. I thought I had walked as swiftly as my thoughts. To be honest, I should tell you that I had been thinking feverishly.

I was so preoccupied that, while I heard the waves lapping, I chose not to look at them. Some things, I knew, continued quite well on their own, without my feeble help. Without stopping, with a faith all their own. I had also ignored passersby, those few remaining souls on the beach at this late hour. And this, too. I had not looked up at the sky even once.

It came to me that I had probably walked a good distance, perhaps several miles. But at some point, without thinking, I had turned back. After all, I was walking east now. When I began, I was going west. Now I was heading home, no doubt about it, like an old horse. And suddenly I found myself laughing again.

And another thing came to me as well. I was limping a bit. My arthritic bones were talking to me again, singing a bit, letting me know they had had quite enough of this walk. Why, if anyone was watching me from inside one of the beach bungalows, they would not see me. They would see a shadow passing. A shadow that limped.

This was not a pleasing thought to me, I tell you. My walk had begun proudly. My walk was one of defiance. In my mind, my walk seethed with a virility unscathed by the years.

The walk had begun after a fight with my wife. We are good, professional fighters, having quarreled for the better part of fifty years. Top that if you can. We are crusaders. The very meaning of a quarrel, over such a great deal of time, has become mythic, with a life of its own. It is a god we serve.

A horse of a habit is what we are. My walks, this walk included, are a kind of sacramental unction. Walks always follow a quarrel. A walk is always just a few steps away. With it comes redemption, but do not ask what kind, or which color. This has always been true to me, but not to my wife.

My wife is not a walker, or at least not after a quarrel. Instead, she prefers to do housework. In particular, she finds dusting to be quite therapeutic. Tabletops, glassware, sea shells, those damned knickknacks she collects. Whatever is near, whatever seems fragile, whatever requires her attention. And, living as we do by the sea, everything acquires a second skin of salty grime.

Because we quarrel so often, our house shines. Our house is the essence of cleanliness, as visitors regularly point out. This has a down side for my wife, though. With everything so clean so much of the time, she is sometimes frustrated after a fresh quarrel. But she presses on, just as I do.

Now my walk is ending. Here, beneath a moon of murky directives, I see our white bungalow with blue trim. I cross the small wooden walkway that leads over the dune to the steps of the house. By now, I know, our house will sparkle. Life will begin again.

Once inside, I will say nothing to her about our quarrel, or my walk. She will refrain from any talk of dusting. She does not need to know about the thoughts I had while I was walking. She does not know how many times I killed her inside my head, and she does not need to know. A thousand deaths, during many walks, over the long, circuitous path of years. This night too, of course. Bloody little murders, all of them, sensational private events, many of them worth a television movie. The thought of our lives, and deaths, portrayed on the screen makes me laugh again.

All things being fair, I am aware that I too have probably been murdered in my absence. She might have killed me while polishing a brass lion bookend. Or perhaps while she scrubbed the tub, trying to erase all trace of my bludgeoning.

But all these murders and motives disappear for the moment. I laugh and the wind carries my laughter across the marshes, toward the bay that glistens bone white with moonlight. I climb the wooden stairs to the house. I'm tired now, and my bones sing an audible dirge.

I can see the light in the bedroom. She has waited up, and the fact of this pleases me greatly.

In spite of my seventy-four years, the light makes me feel suddenly young again. How can I explain such a thing? But it is what I truly feel. The pain in my legs begins to disappear. With half a sprint, I take the few remaining steps.

I open the door. The house smells fresh and new. Stepping inside, I wonder how I could have ever left.

WOMAN CARRYING CLOUDS AND SKY

She lives alone, just up the street. No question about that. But why she lives alone relates to a time before when she lived with someone. Years ago, long before I ever laid eyes on her. Some man, a grease monkey I've been told, had her for awhile. Maybe he wasn't much, and maybe he was. But the fact is that she had never been with a man before. Holding hands through the night. All that.

It seems they weren't too far into things when he began taking swipes at her. In the air around her head, more and more connecting with her face. She took it, she didn't know any better. Nothing to compare it with, you understand. Those little bird bones in her face cracked and hurt.

Time passed, as they say. After enough of this, she wanted to be done with this guy. She told him to leave. But the problem was that he wouldn't go. Wouldn't budge. He hung on like a lingering flu. And his swipes in the air got deadlier too.

He didn't have a job. Fact is, he hadn't worked since the day she took him inside her house like a stray. He never worked a lick. In time, I'm told, his grease monkey fingernails looked like new.

He drank beer and ate whatever she cooked for him, and in the afternoons he watched the soap operas through bleary eyes. Late afternoons, things got special. Late afternoons, he'd crawl between her designer sheets and wait for her. She was coming home from work for that. All that. God knows there wasn't a lot of glory in it. Mind you, that's not my opinion, just what I've been told. It's probably true, though.

After awhile, even Mr. Grease Monkey got tired of this. He left one day while she was away at work. He left and took most things of worth with him. He didn't leave her much, maybe some stains on the Calvin Klein sheets. Not a lot, by most standards. She must have sat around sad in that house, across town from here. She was trying to decide what to do next, you know. I'd do the same thing. 'Course, I'd never get myself in such a jam, and neither would you, but that's another matter.

It was about then that she moved into the little house up the street. She started all over again, on her lonesome, though. And you have to give her credit. She could have put her head in an oven or something, I don't know. Sometimes, when things turn bad, people go straight to hell. It happens. You know it too.

But she's made the best of it, as far as any of us can tell. In the time she's been on our street, she hasn't brought home any more strays. It's anyone's guess, but I figure she's learned her lesson on that score.

Does she hate herself for what happened to her? Well, for sure she hates that grease monkey, no matter where he went, no matter whose sheets he's soiling tonight. But she doesn't tell us how she feels. She stays to herself, and that's how we like it around here. The neighbors think she's off, and I have to concur. There's no evidence to the contrary, you see.

She drives like a banshee down the street when she's coming or going. Get the kids and cats and dogs out of the street, she's coming through. Fifty miles an hour on our little street. Maybe she thinks she's being watched. Maybe she's afraid that grease monkey will try to follow her home.

No one's seen him around, though. I figure he's warming someone else's sheets about now.

That stuff, it's habit for some. He's probably toasting his toes, waiting for the time to move on again. No matter where he is, he's still got some kind of grip on her. She's really not in her right mind, it seems to most of us. She'll never look you in the eye. Makes you feel like you've done something wrong.

Makes you think she's expecting you to crawl in her window one night with a knife between your teeth.

It's creepy, sure. And there's the wigs, too, each of them another fact of the matter. She has a half-dozen, all colors, and she rotates them. She'll be out watering the azaleas, a long brown wig swaying this way and that while she's looking up and down the street for something.

But here's the worst. One day, she came walking up the street this way. In a blonde wig, and carrying a full-length mirror. I don't know where she was going. None of my business. But it was strange because she kept that mirror facing away from her. She wouldn't look into it. Wouldn't take that chance, I guess.

I watched her from my window when she passed down below. I saw clouds and blue sky reflected in that mirror. She carried it over her shoulder, like Jesus at Golgotha. The same mood. You know? The grim stuff. That was it for me.

Will it get any better for her? No, it's probably too late. Can it get worse? Sure, there's always plenty of time for that.

COLLECTRESS

In the field, her horses. Beyond them, the lone buffalo. Here, near the house, chickens and geese. Puppies, hamsters, multiplying cats. Caged birds, all kinds, most colors, many songs.

She owns it all. She fills space with everything she imagines herself to be, at the moment. But now, after so many seasons, her purpose is fading. The menagerie grows, but she no longer remembers why.

He approaches when evening comes. Walks up the road, carries sacks of grain. A twanging tongue, a Southern boy. Something about him intrigues her. Each man who came before held a fascination. For a time. When it passed, the road led them away again.

This man coming up the road, this man will do. For now. Until her fancy changes. Again. Until he no longer serves the purpose for which he was acquired.

SUNSET OR AN OLD SHOE

(After Carver)

However you wish to say it, in brief lines, or long like the slow river flow, subjects are always the same.

Sunset or an old shoe.

The former come regularly, spectacular and not, each of them begging memory's favor.

As for shoes, some tell stories. Abandoned in closets, they are paint-speckled and dusty. Arranged in the right way, they seem to walk like the ghosts of wild old men.

ACOLYTES

Fresh light washes across the churchyard. Slivers of dawn pierce the stained-glass windows of the church, and of the rectory where Father Dominic is waking. I imagine him rolling over in bed, excavating the sheets for a way back into the night. Then, heavy with regret, he arises. Eyes still sleep shut, he stumbles to the bathroom to wash his face.

With only five minutes until five o'clock Mass, he flushes the toilet with one hand while grabbing his cassock off a hook with the other. The idiot girl from the rectory tells me this.

The sacristy at dawn is quiet as Stonehenge. Already we are there waiting, Quinlan and myself, sipping wine, munching unconsecrated hosts. We wear black cassocks and starched, white lace surplices. Quinlan stands by the window, watching for Father Dominic's approach. We may ditch breakfast prematurely if he arrives too soon.

Comes a faint sound, of whispers talking among themselves from the other side of the altar, a sound slipping from the dank church where dawn is assembling. I look out, see three old women, without faces and buried in shawls, huddled in the dim light. There is no one else, just the women and their tattered voices. I think of witches, of secrets told for so many generations that the voices have died and only whispers remain.

We put away the wine and hosts. I replace Father Dominic's wine level mark on the bottle with another of my own. We pace, waiting for Dominic. He's late again. Quinlan passes the time by spit-shining his shoes with a cassock hem. It goes without a mention, that Dominic has had another hard night.

Outside, the chimes resound over the night-battered neighborhood. Lights are coming on in small, working class homes. Men emerge from them in undershirts to retrieve the morning paper, then go back inside to start the coffee and wake the wife. Ham, eggs and sex, a working-class fugue.

Where I am, in the sacristy, I cannot see Old Mr. Joe playing his morning medley on the steeple bells. But if I close my eyes I can see him there, an emaciated frame swinging and jerking, a marionette dangling in ropes, deaf and manic and laughing to himself. Once he brought his grandson to see the bells, the room where he worked, where the ropes dangled, waiting to be pulled. The boy looked long and hard up that steeple, and then pointed to the belfry. Smiling, Mr. Joe then led the boy up the steepest of stairs for a better look. The old man collapsed, halfway there. Now it has been years since Mr. Joe has actually seen the bells. He speaks with them, from a distance, in a language of ropes.

His bells are thunder in Father Dominic's hungover head. He stands in the rectory kitchen, shouting curses between gulps of orange juice crushed by the idiot girl. He thinks about the woman from the night before, and tells himself it was worth it. No one hears him but the idiot girl, shy, standing to the side. She tells us all about it, of course, she who will also show us her breasts if asked.

In a few moments the bells go quiet and a broad silence breathes in the church. The faceless shawls emit the clicking noise of chattering teeth and fervent rosaries. On the walls, saints awaken one by one, in glass, in gradual light. Quinlan and I are pacing, our words stumbling from wine-thickened tongues. There is nothing to be done about our breath but to pray, an unlikelihood at best. Sometimes, when he is in the foulest of moods, Dominic will stop to smell our breath.

At last he appears, his own cassock trailing in the air behind him. He disappears into the vestment room. We wait in anticipation, in fear that we might fall if we try to walk. When Dominic appears again, he has become a glittering image in his Vatican City threads. The door sweeps shut behind him, and I think of Dorothy Lamour.

It is time for Mass to begin. Quinlan rings the small bell and the tinkling sound shatters the silence. The three witches rise in a mass of clockwork grey.

Our prayers rise to touch flaking frescoes, up into the thin air of residual Gregorian chants.

Our prayers sound surprisingly sincere, young enough not to be tarnished. Dominic watches us. Choose your acolytes and choirboys early on, another old priest had told him once. A soprano is best, and multi-faceted.

The old priest often gave crustaceous advice, his cigar smoke accumulating in layers on the rectory ceiling, a fifth glass of cognac dangling from his liver spotted hand. Gone now, into smoke and incense, laid to rest in the consecrated ground of all humble servants. Now Dominic offers a prayer to the old priest's spirit, raising a chalice aloft. I watch his unshaven face curving, contorting in gold distortions.

At communion, Dominic holds the host low for the kneeling Quinlan, who unknowingly presents a wine-colored tongue. Recognizing the evidence of the boy's transgression, Dominic places a host on Quinlan's tongue, then lets a finger slide down his throat. Lost in their reverie, the shawls see none of this, nor do they notice an acolyte running from the altar, vomiting into his surplice. Wisely, then, I refuse the body of Christ. Dominic eyes me warily, looks bemused, then walks to the altar rail where the shawls are clicking still, waiting for manna.

DURING THE FLOOD

"Put it there," I told them.

So the two of them brought it in and slowly hoisted it onto the table. They had found it washed up on the Moose River bank at sunset. It was no matter of delicacy as they let it down, roughly. It spread out across the hard wooden surface. There, in the light, we saw it plainly, and I thought I heard it sigh as if it had finally given up, completely.

"What you gonna do with it?" one asked.

"I haven't decided," I told him.

"You could eat it," said the other, his lips all in a snarl.

"Maybe cook it, and sell souvenirs. You know, strips?"

"You're a real sicko, Jack," the first one said, but they both got to laughing.

They looked like brothers, or real close cousins, I could see. Low foreheads. I didn't want to know. We were river people, all of us, and everything that came with it.

"You want us to stay?" Jack asked.

I thought about it. How I would probably feel being left alone all night with it there on the table. Music and shadows, real and not, and me not able to sleep.

"I guess," I mumbled. Hell, I wasn't sure what I wanted.

"You *guess*?"

"I mean," I said, "maybe one of you stay. Just until dawn anyway."

"Which one?" he asked, not looking me in the eye.

I could see it wasn't going to be easy. Neither of them said another word. They looked at each other, then at the floor. Afraid to stay, and afraid to say so. It got real quiet for a minute. Then, they started moving, backing out the open door. I knew I was on my own.

Outside, it was still raining.

SPANNING

(After John Cheever)

You feared bridges. In this, you were not alone. It goes for us all, fearing not what a bridge is, but where it leads us. Beneath the steel and concrete pretense howls a muffled song of dread. How will we change for having gone, spanned a bay, crossed a river with shanty towns on either bank, passed above the dried creeks of summer?

Sometimes, fear is misdirected. You believed that angels appeared, celestial wayfarers who stood at the ends of bridges. They would climb inside your car, guide you, steady the heart and mind. That way, the ride would be made safe. Bearable. Maybe so.

But what did you really know about angels? I say you should be careful of some of them. You can tell which ones, but you must look very closely. Their eyes are vacant and their faces are frightening and dirty. Loose ebony threads cling to their arms, their soft pale wings. It even collects in their hair.

I think it is those angels you need to fear. Not bridges. A bridge is only a way to prepare us for the eventual long, ultimate spanning. Then, there will be no sound of water below us, only the tattered dry song that rides the wind through the bones of animals scattered along every riverbank. Thirsty, they came to drink, guided by some angels. You and I, we must find another way.

THE FIRE PRIESTS

After another car passed, we set to work. Poured gasoline, can after can, on the asphalt. Not smoking, any of us. Holding our breath. Fumes stung our skin worse than the winter wind.

This was our practice run, on the old farm-to-market road. If all went well, the plan was to douse I-20 next. It lay across the land like a silver promise. Waiting.

Someone shouted in the dark as the match was struck. We ran like deer. Over a fence, across a night blue field of high grass.

Behind us, the world was on fire. Ahead of us, in the distance, lights from a farmhouse glowed like our past and our future.

THE SEA CHANGES

Here, this night, Alexander's letters rest on my desk. They are scattered here and there, in small piles around the room, on sills and shelves and the floor. When I walk, I feel I am walking across his heart.

But he won't mind. After all, Alexander does not expect me to remain seated at my desk, reading and re-reading his letters, as if there was nothing else to do. He would not want to limit my life in that way.

Still, there is no getting around it, how much time I do spend on his letters. They are so pure, from deep inside him. Some I have memorized. All I have taken to heart. A few of them, the most private letters of all, are curled in the pockets of old pants. I carry them with me on long walks. When I sleep in old pants, Alexander's letters are with me to walk through my dreams. In this way, they are like directives.

All the letters, who can know how many, are growing older. Like myself, like Alexander. The yellowed envelopes are pressed inside yet another, even larger envelope made of time and dust, of old light and dimming dreams. Looking at them, and at all that is now my life, some nights I imagine the letters to be layers of Alexander himself.

The first layer must always be memory. It dances and hides, and is the hardest to know for certain. The next layer must be time, but these days that is but another uncertainty that runs a course, maybe oblivious to me, perhaps in spite of me.

No doubt there are other layers, many of them, but they are not so important here and now. Memory and time, they must matter most. I put the one with the other, make a ball of them, then roll it from one palm to the other. This is how I try to make sense of Alexander, and why he matters so much to me.

This is a difficult thing to know. So much time has drifted by and away. Time, friend, is river water. Time is wind. It is a force that prevents things from staying as they are for very long. Time is Alexander, or he is time. I suspect the truth lies somewhere between the two.

I like to think of him still young and unchanged, like the sea mountains where he lives. I close my eyes and imagine him there, in a small house nestled between blue sky and low, scraping clouds. He is gathered in the hard hands and arms of those mountains.

I think of him at night, perhaps frightened in that silent place of wavy, liquid wind that rushes through crag and bone. I like to think his letters are born of this same silence. And fear too, perhaps.

I wonder why he is condemned to live in a place most would call dire and forlorn. Here, so far away from that, I wait to see his postmark, a gnarled oak root strangling a snake. His letters are strikes against the silence. They are a way to confront evil, to defeat it.

Each letter, when it does arrive, shatters the silence of my sea room. Through the afternoon I watch the sun, crimson with longing, as it plunges into the cool, wide bay. I can't change any of it. I say nothing, not to people in the village, not even to myself. I have, in fact, spoken to no one in years.

Yes, I am alone here. If I am in some kind of hereafter, so be it. I have no qualms about it. What matters most now are the letters from Alexander. I shift in my chair in the cold night, the dark watery expanse all around me. I feel the waves carrying me so sensuously, from one palm to the other.

I continue to write letters to Alexander, and hope that he awaits them with the same longing as I do his. I try to imagine the delighted look on his face when he receives them, how he holds the pages in his hands.

When I write, I print well, taking great care. When a letter is complete, I add my seal, the gnarled oak root strangling a snake. Tomorrow, I tell myself, I will mail it, and I truly believe this will happen. I place the letter on one of many piles that only grow, on sills and shelves, on the floor.

INSIDE

I have a city inside me. You can't see it, but it's there. Believe me. Evenings, it stirs. Rumbles. Thrashes about. It has its own sound, I tell you, like nothing else. A kind of roar. What's worse, nothing I can do or say will make it stop.

Late evenings, I have visions. Apparitions, all kinds. Do not ask what they are. They're bloody, I know that much. Some come headless. Because of this, I have lost sight of other things. People, pleasures, peacefulness. All the things I took for granted, in fact. Everything I thought was ordinary.

And this. The city inside me is brimming with flowers. All kinds. So many flowers there is not room for them all. Or their colors, pressing into each other. There's hardly room for fragrance.

There is also rage, without end. Rage can hold this city in its hand, control it building by building. I won't tell you about that, about the pain. Or the wails and shouts and wasted tears. I won't say what I know about the secrets that rise from smokestacks screaming into the sky. You don't want to know anyway.

But the monster is something you should want to know about. Somehow, he sleeps through it all, this monster. He coils at the bottom of my brain. Deep, so very deep, asleep in tunnels below the city inside me. Oh yes, he's there. No doubt about it. He sleeps and doesn't worry about any of this, I swear. Dreaming. As if he's never known a thing but sleep. Here and now, maybe for always.

When I am tired of thinking about the city inside me, I sometimes consider the monster. I wonder what would happen if he awakened. If he did, well...

The usual worries, somewhere between bloom and rage. If he should wake, things will change. Drift. Spiral into another sensibility, perhaps. I can't be sure. Nothing is certain here. Only that the monster sleeps. What would happen? It is something I would rather not know.

I tell you this because I have seen him awaken in others. How he stretches his foul shadow. And the others, they go it as best they can. You see them, lost and grumbling, half-dead, wandering the earth from one city to the next. You see the monster staring from their eyes. His sadness, utter and complete. That is what I mean.

With that sadness there is also something else. It is what they all say, the question they ask others along the road. This road, that road, any and all roads will do. They want to know if the monster will ever turn over, if he will ever go back to sleep again.

THE BUS

Would you mind if I shared your park bench? No? Thank you, then. Yes, this is quite nice. I love Chapultepec. You must also love it. Am I right? Yes? It keeps us coming back, don't you think? Like an old song. Yes, that is how I like to imagine it. Like an old song. Some kind of lure about it.

Tell me, do you know parks in Europe? No? Well, I'm sorry that you don't. But if you are very careful, there is still time for that.

Why? Because I have to tell you something. If a bus stops here, pretend you were expecting it. Yes, I am quite sure that this is no ordinary stop. You see, at my age, the unusual becomes the pattern. I have seen or heard most everything.

For now, I can tell you this. I feel quite certain that the infamous bus will be making a stop here soon. Why? Because I know. Last night, I dreamed it stopped again. Oh, it's always stopping somewhere, you might say. And I would agree.

This time, however, I saw it. I was, in fact, a kind of witness. I see very well in my dreams. The tired old brain doesn't forget all the things it has lost. Memories, sight itself, the all of it.

My dreams are the colors of carnivals. I don't know how it is for the rest of the blind, but when I dream, colors are an electric bright. They intensify. You cannot imagine. Trees are a glowing green fire. Buildings pulse. A compensation, you say? Maybe. You could say that.

But let me tell you about my dream. I was walking down Reforma, taking my usual cane-tapping stroll through the kaleidoscope. Everything lovely. Beyond loveliness, really. A song in my heart. Then, I heard the bus coming. It came close by, then veered away. Passed on.

No stopping for me, of course. But listening to it pass, I

decided that, in an odd way, it reminded me of an ambulance. They are always around, you know. They pass you for someone else most of the time. But there's no doubt about one thing. One day or night, one will stop at your door. Or at your feet.

As I was saying, I was old news for the bus. But I knew it would stop for someone else. Unexpectedly, always. But if it should stop here today, there is something I need to ask you. A small favor. Would you be kind enough to lead me up the steps?

You're very kind, thank you. Oh, and one more thing. An even smaller request. Don't lead me so quickly that I might miss a step. Some do, you know, always ready to be rid of a blind man. No, I ask you to do it calmly, like you've done it before. A thousand times. There is salvation in this, I assure you.

Salvation? No, the temporal kind, you might say. Some say it's just as good. But remember this. When we get on the bus, don't look anyone in the eye. *No one.* I warn you, don't look at anything in particular. Do you understand?

No matter how much you might want to look at something, say a woman's thighs, try to resist.

Why? Because it's a giveaway, that sort of thing. And the thieves are wise to it. You must be on guard. Always. You must be very careful. If you're not...

Listen to me. I am not just another madman who floats through this park. I tell you all this for a reason. Once I too was young. It's not so impossible to imagine, is it? In fact, I was about your age when it happened. You don't mind my touching your face, do you? Hands, in my case, are like map readers.

It happened, like I said, when I was still young. And on the bus. I had been sitting on a park bench, the other side of Chapultepec. Thinking too much, probably. Worrying. About money, and the fact that I didn't have much. Or, considering ways to patch things up with my girlfriend. Oh, we were a battlefield, but it kept things molten between us.

Thinking I would buy her some flowers, or take her to a film. Thinking so hard that I only vaguely heard the bus approach. The tires squealed, the door swung open. I was young, muddled and naive. Unsuspecting. I stood up, an uncertain general making plans for peace with my girl. I stood up and got on the bus, by God.

By then it was already too late, but I couldn't know that. The bus pulled away. We moved through the traffic. I saw the park out the window. Every blink a postcard. Couples walking hand in hand, birds landing in trees, the venders, the very pace of this place. I took it in, the film of it all.

I was such an easy target. They came up on either side of me and held me down. I was powerless. And they did it. They cut out my eyes.

Quickly, so quickly. The film I was watching suddenly turned on its side, blurred, then was gone. There was nothing but blackness. And the promise of much more blackness to come, of course.

Now you understand these dark glasses, and this white cane I call my staff. Who knows, maybe I am some kind of prophet. But this staff doesn't divide an ocean. No, this staff divides the darkness.

Last night, as I told you, I dreamed all this. About you. I walked through the kaleidoscope of the city. In the park, I decided to sit down and rest. I found a bench, like this one.

I sat and listened to the sounds of traffic. My hearing is so intense. At times I feel like the avenues are inside my head, that cars are driving on the inside of my skull. It is another kind of compensation, I know.

Then, I heard someone approach. A youthful gait. A young man came and sat down next to me. His greeting was slight and muffled. Uncommitted, so like your own.

I could tell he was thinking hard about something. I could

almost hear his thoughts. Money? His girlfriend? We didn't discuss it. We were both so busy, watching our own films. Then, I heard the bus. Coming at us, bearing down hard.

Oh, I knew it wasn't stopping for me. I was old news. But this young man was unsuspecting, always the best prey. When the bus stopped, he stood up, not thinking where he was going. Or what would happen after he took a seat and the bus began moving again.

That is how my dream ended. Me wanting to tell him, to warn him. I wanted to shake him loose somehow. But I couldn't. My dreams, no matter how brilliant their colors, always leave me tongue-tied. So my only choice was to go with him, follow him onto the bus. Later, when the eye thieves were done with him, I could console him. Maybe I could lead him home.

Now, do you understand? Good. Here, take my glasses. I won't need them. Wear them when the bus stops. Keep looking straight ahead, like I told you. Don't give yourself away.

With any luck, they'll think they're already done with you. Why, if God smiles, they'll go after someone else.

MEN IN A TRUCK

I knew they were around. Had been around, all afternoon. Something in the air. Early on, this morning, in fact. There was some talk of them. Someone had even seen them around dawn in a nearby neighborhood.

At the vegetable stand on my street, people lowered their voices. They're coming today, one woman said as she halfheartedly gathered tomatoes. She said it was her son's birthday, and then she began to cry. No one said anything to this. People nodded and looked away with marble faces. My own skin felt hard, and I was glad I could not feel my heart.

Late, getting on evening, the smell came through my closed shutters. I was sitting in the dark, on the side of my bed. Not doing much. Anticipating, that's for sure. I must have been in the middle of something. Writing a letter. A poem. Writing a will. All in my head.

Whatever I had been doing, I stopped. The smell was like ether. Clammy. If a smell alone could kill senses, this was it. I sat like a zombie, unable to move, in the dark. I waited for it to be over. I waited to hear the men in a truck pass below, to be done with our street.

A knock on the door. Twice. My landlady, the old dear, let herself in finally. Her eyes were wild, like a frightened cow. They're going house by house tonight, she said. Her voice was a fluttering kind of thing. Something new, even for them, I said. Oh yes, she said. Oh yes.

But it wasn't until past midnight that they came to my door. I didn't try to stop them. I had even left the door ajar, a way of saying I had nothing to hide. I had heard the widow woman next door begging them not to spray her photographs, her old fake jewels. And I heard a slamming noise, like something frail gone flying. Then a loud bump, like she hit the floor. It got very quiet.

They came in, about six of them, wearing masks. Burly, storm trooper types. Two of them carried the spray cans. The others began digging, thrashing about. They could have been looking for anything, I knew. I let them go. I'm not ashamed to say it. I let it all go.

What about those books, one wanted to know. Which books, I asked him. Most of them, probably, he sneered. No, all of them, said another. Before I could say anything else, they got busy.

They took large handfuls of books and hurled them to the floor. Hard, like they wanted to be done with them. They held the cans high and sprayed those books good. I thought, for as long as I live and read, I'll be smelling this night.

The smell was quite intense. I was full of it. I felt like a soft rubber man. I thought about the widow woman falling down next door. I wondered if she woke. I must have passed out. I didn't hear the men leave. Never heard their truck leaving our street.

THE WOUND

You've kept it bandaged properly all day and into the night. Not to protect it, or to be socially responsible, but to hide it. From *them*. The wound has knowledge others want.

Now, beneath the late night lamp, the wind singing out the window, you unwrap it. The bandage unfolds slowly, like memory flayed. That done, you see it clearly. With two fingers you pry it open afresh. You ignore the new blood and peer inside. You can see the passage, even glimmers of light visible from the other side.

Slowly, with utmost care, you begin crawling, pushing, never stopping to consider the impossibility of it, to climb inside oneself. If you stop to think about it, you know the magic will evaporate. You pass through the red forest, beneath the white mountain range, obsessed with the concept of *beyond*.

By the time you stop to rest you are already in another country. In a town, in fact. You wander the streets which are filled with people carrying balloons. Music in the air. A fair of sorts, though you have no idea what is being celebrated.

In any case, you do not feel a need to be part of the festivities. At random, you select a building and go inside. Climb what seems like endless spiral staircases until you feel you have finally escaped the noises below. You open a door and find yourself standing in an office. Desks, files, many machines. You find what you are looking for, a desk where a man sits, playing with a scab on his arm. You watch as he pulls it off, then holds his own wound for you to see. You do see it, the unbearable sadness, in his eyes. You have seen it in your own eyes.

You feel an unspoken kinship with him. So it does not surprise you when he pries his old wound open with a shiny brass letter opener. You step forward to see it more clearly. He is making the passage clear. All you need to do is to decide if you want to continue the journey alone, or if you want to take the man along with you.

You search his eyes for trust. It's there or not, in one person or another, one town to the next. It can make all the difference in the world. Trusting, yes or no.

You finally decide he cannot be trusted. It's nothing more that intuition, but it is strong. You back away as he begins to crawl inside his own wound. In seconds, he's gone.

You sit down in the chair at his desk. You begin shuffling unfamiliar papers in an unknown language. You attempt to appear proper and professional. But you cannot ignore the letter opener left there with blood on the tip.

You pick it up and run it along your arm. It grazes the skin so gracefully. Then, as though it had a mind all its own, the letter opener dives into the flesh. You pry open the new wound, see a dim light in the distance. Through another red forest, over the next white mountain range. Always a promise of a civilized world. *Beyond.* Always seeming closer than it is in reality. Than it can be.

But a slim hope is better than none. You bend over. You go head first.

DEAR FRANCISCO

...and because you ask, and only for this reason. Otherwise, I would keep my mouth where it belongs, shut tightly here in a room in my dead father's house. I fear things, being called upon to explain myself, for instance. But because you ask...

... and because in your youth you are waist deep in naivete, and perhaps because I do not have much longer to live, and if it is true that you are some kind of brother to me as our mothers were one and the same woman, for reasons that simply are, that exist not for me or you or anyone, mothers included, reasons that fester in shadows or fall like hail from skies quite unlike those here.

I don't know why, despite my age and travels, but I shall do my best to be honest in my remarks, to be a truthful witness to what I have seen in this regard, concerning your question about women in windows.

No, it makes no difference, the color of their skin, or hair or eyes, or stockings or nail polish. Allow none of this to enter into it. Even at your tender age, Francisco, you must know that most women are quite unlike those sitting in windows.

Simply being a woman does not suggest a kinship, you see. No, what I have discovered, both in time and travel, is what the women in windows have in common with each other. Let's not get into shutters or lace curtains or beveled glass, oh no, as those will only take you further from the truth of the women you mentioned.

What goes on in their minds? Well, it goes and goes, as they remain in their windows for many years. I'm only speculating, searching for an answer for you. They are always thinking, if only because they are always hoping. One never gets very far without the other, it seems.

I think this is at the crux of it, to simply insist on hope when chances are so very slim, when hell itself seems a much easier thing to grasp. Hope that someone will come, rescue them, and take them away.

Someone, they imagine, who stands in a hotel room in Valencia or Estoril, preparing himself, shaving, nipping brandy, generally primping, God knows, maybe even singing, a fire smoldering in his loins. But the women do not realize that this someone is also thinking about being done with them quickly, being finished and gone again, to Miami or San Juan, where this someone imagines this more or less repeating itself, albeit with variations.

The women... No, allow me to simplify this. I shall make them one woman. This woman, she sits waiting. Her window is her perch. Somewhere on the wide rolling sea of her hope is this chasm, neither tidy nor grand. She is a swimmer on this sea. Forgive me if the metaphorical aspects of this seem tired and shopworn, but I do believe this is an apt description of how she imagines herself.

I consider her like that, seashells and urchins nesting in her hair. Have I told you that at night I sometimes watch for our mother in the sky? If I am drunk enough, I imagine she is a constellation, her legs spread wide enough for meteors to shoot through.

Our mother or this woman, it doesn't matter so much. What is important here is that she does not look at the sky spread out above, or the immense blue water in any direction. Instead, she will be staring down into that chasm I mentioned.

She does this because she knows how the days drift like the hours, like the wind. Here and now, hours will do. Every hour she has known, in fact, so much like every man she's known alone, the pair of them swaying this way and that on the sky of her bed.

Poised or not, most of her thinking has to do with the time she spends alone, for days untouched by anyone, not a solitary human hand, even a fingertip. But needing to be, of course.

And, knowing how very long a day can be, how long this kind of waiting can span.

So this, my Francisco, is why, when looking in windows, I humbly suggest that it is better if you find an old woman, preferably a very old one, looking back. Dreadful though she may be, there will be a smile beginning to cross her face. It is because she sees you.

She believes her lengthy dream is coming true. And you, being a better dreamer, wake up. It's the sensible thing to do, believe me. Wake up, and when you dream again it will be in another city, a different window, another woman.

I should tell you one thing you may not have learned yet. Did you know that the most beautiful women in windows are really skeletons in disguise? It's true. Kiss their flesh and it evaporates. It becomes cold bones, the clickety-clack stuff. There's no waking from that dream once you've been embraced.

And do I need to warn you also that it may be our mother looking back at you from a window? Good, I thought not. But sometimes you can be certain of nothing in these matters. Heritage, in our case, is a string with many ends.

But because you did not ask my opinion on the afterlife, or about the women in the windows in hell, I think I will refrain from discussing these matters until a time when you feel up to it. For now, this seems to be a good place to...

Ciao,

Vincenzo

THE WORLD ENDS HERE

Here is where they have ended up, off a sand street. In this place, up from the marina. Sea turtles, normally with such an exquisite sense of direction, punctual to the point of a star. Now, if they have any god left at all, it is this snaggletoothed woman who comes out of her hut to greet us.

We stand in the side yard and ask if we might view the turtles. The old woman laughs. She thinks we must have little to do in the late afternoon. But she says this time of day is best. Watch them come awake, she tells us. She says they are preparing for the night highway that reaches down to them from the sky. With this knowledge, we follow her to the turtle tank.

There are two of them, side by side, in the cement space. The water brackish, it churns a bit with the small feeble motions they make with their sea diving flippers. They are unable to turn in the small tank. It must be a mad kind of torture, with just enough room to raise their heads, to study the dimensions of confinement. Just enough to see the night sky, always so generous with directives.

Tonight the stars will drift overhead, but they will remain here, bumping the concrete walls of a small universe. For them, the world ends here.

WOMAN WAITING FOR A SHIP

In the port city, we are waiting. Gathered down at the docks, we steal food from one another. We fear falling asleep, maybe losing our places in line. You don't want to know about the air. Imagine the worst, then you'll have it. The smell of burnt hell.

Some say the ship, if it comes, is made of skin, layer after layer, keeping it afloat. But the one-eyed woman, who claims to have waited longest and who still prays all day, says the ship is made of souls. I say, that's too much prayer talking. Still, we all admit to some of that, the credo mythic. Else why would we be huddled here, rain-soaked, half-starved, breathing fetid air, waiting for a barge, a raft, an ark, whatever we imagine?

A week ago, it seems, I stood up to leave. All this. And go home, I thought, to wherever it had been, however I recalled the place.

Yet I knew that was all years ago now, back down a washed out road, so to speak, that no longer existed. I pretended otherwise. So, like that, my body filthy, lice hopping, my clothes rotting, I got up. I announced I would wait no longer.

I even took a few steps. Some east, some west. Then, I stopped. On this wharf alone, ten thousand eyes were watching me. Across the water, in torchlight, I saw the others. Then the laughter, all of it, began. It did not stop until I found my place again, sat down cross-legged, my head between my knees. I was too tired to care, too weak to get up again.

Nearby, the one-eyed woman continued to laugh, long after the others had stopped. Looking at her, I knew it could be worse. Ship of skin, of old souls, however it was, I knew I could have been in her place. Could be her, in fact. One eye on the docks, the other grazing the horizon for the ship. Never knowing which vision was better, or which might be true. Seeing and smelling it longer than me, maybe longer than I had been alive.

CHOIRS

She promised them the songs of angels, so how could they resist? That morning in the plaza, the song mistress gathered all the village children. She raised their voices toward heaven. They dropped the guttural sound of their native tongue. Their voices blended so sweetly, the words themselves became like honey. Parents, none of whom could believe this rare and wonderful feat, stood in the street, waiting for the angels to descend from heaven.

But no angels appeared. Instead, the songs the children sang were so sweet that the rich honey of their voices began to flow from inside them. It pooled at their feet and began spreading, wider and wider around them, deeper and deeper, until they could no longer move, until their small heads disappeared beneath waves of the golden liquid.

The sweetness had no end. Eventually it drowned the parents, then flowed through the narrow streets, overwhelming the small shops and the people inside them. It moved on with a cruel mind of its own. By noon, the entire village was lost to the lyrical flood.

When evening fell, the song mistress spread her bony wings from hell and took flight, already on her way to the next village.

TOUCH

When winter came and wind was harsh and the ground white, they kept to themselves. For months, cloistered in their ruddy huts with nothing but themselves and the frozen food they had gathered.

It began by holding each other, afraid of what might happen next. They touched each other so innocently, a way to comfort one another. But this happened during what became an unending winter, when the ground remained hard and white for years. They touched each other, rubbing their skin hard to keep the blood flowing.

The first blood spewed forth unexpectedly. They had rubbed themselves raw, and there was no stopping it. Before anyone could think of what to do, it was too late.

Sadly, the hands could understand none of this. They continued to caress and, in a strange way, to hope. In a very short time, there was nothing left of any of them, only their weary hands. They kept on.

Bone to bone and terribly desperate, they inadvertently sparked a fire so intense that it consumed the bones, the ruddy huts, the hard white earth, the memory of blood.

Even the sense of touch was lost. Some say it did not return for five thousand years. Others insist we are living without it still.

NOTES FROM CONCH MOUNTAIN

They were obsessed with dreams. Each morning, islanders would gather in the plaza or at the conch mountain, taking turns telling dreams. Usually these dreams were fresh, from the night before. Sometimes they were fabrications, or dressed up versions of earlier dreams that had failed to ignite imaginations. This was allowed, as it was considered wrong not to make use of a dream that had even an ounce of worth in it.

On the island, one was considered a fool or a lunatic if he dreamed little. Or worse, if he never dreamed at all. Some found it necessary to invent dreams to retain a measure of self-respect. Much time and effort was given in this pursuit most mornings upon waking.

Dreams were a test of both will and imagination. One was forced to delve deeply, even into the soul, for a dream magnificent enough to impress others. No one discussed this individual process with anyone else. Dreams and their origins were considered a private matter, between Maker and dreamer.

Old Mendoza, the island Elder, was down near the docks at the conch mountain every morning. He would hold dream court. Like the others too old to go out fishing, he spent his time mending nets. Most of the menders were blind, as was Mendoza.

Islanders respected Mendoza and the other menders, placing them just below the Virgin Mary in their deity. In Mendoza's case, this was because of age, but there was another reason as well. They held him in such high esteem because of all the songs he knew by heart. Thousands of songs, more than anyone else. He was revered most, however, for the fact that he dreamed more than anyone else on the island.

Old Mendoza claimed he had as many as a hundred dreams

on a given night. He could easily relate a dozen dreams in a row, just as he sang all those songs without forgetting a word.

Once, and no one could remember when, Mendoza declared that, the older a person is, the more he dreams and the better he can recall the dreams.

Each morning, dozens of children ran through the sandy streets to the conch mountain. They fought for a place to sit nearest the old man as he recited his dreams from the night before. The children, as well as the adults, learned more from old Mendoza that they ever could from books. At the school run by Maestra Gabriella, the same material was taught year after year from the same book, the only copy of which belonged to her and was a Bible she had once received from a now deceased uncle who lived on the mainland.

In her own way, Maestra Gabriella was considered learned. She was revered for her knowledge, much the same as Old Mendoza was for his memory, on an island where there was so little learning to be had.

And while these two never agreed on anything, their opinions were often sought. Islanders carefully weighed what they had to say on a given subject, allowing it to volley back and forth until it landed in a place of decision. For more serious disagreements, Maestra Gabriella had been known to bow to Old Mendoza, for she too revered his age and was too young to compete with it.

This is why the matter of the child was brought to both of them. An island woman had borne a child which her husband said was not his own. Violence erupted in their house, and soon included their entire street. The Indian priest, who was summoned to baptize the child, was the first to enter the house. Unwilling to act alone, the priest summoned Maestra Gabriella and Old Mendoza. Together, the three of them would decide how best to settle the father's grievance.

While a crowd of curious onlookers waited outside in the street, the tribunal inspected first the mother, then the enraged husband, and finally the newborn child. The Indian priest said it made no difference who had fathered the child as long as the baby was created by the Maker.

Maestra Gabriella was next to give her opinion. She said she saw no reason to be any more excited by this particular birth than any other on the island. Given the fact that everyone looked alike, it could surely make no difference. She concluded by saying that the real father was Juan Cantos, an island man known for his paternal prowess.

She also told the husband of the unfaithful wife that he should forgive her, and that he should thank Juan Cantos. After all, he now had a namesake who might be as virile as Juan Cantos himself. The husband seemed agreeable to all this until Old Mendoza stood up to give his opinion.

Mendoza said that since the child was made by parents not joined together by the Maker, it could never become a child of the Maker, or anyone else. The baby would have to be put to death.

The mother wept in the small room where they all stood. She said she knew that Old Mendoza was right, and that she knew this was going to happen. The night before giving birth, she had dreamed of wolves feasting on a newborn lamb.

No one in the room could question a dream so vivid and so very timely, so they all agreed to do away with the baby. It was covered with a small mountain of pillows and suffocated. Each of them took a turn holding the pillows in place so that no one person would be held responsible in the eyes of the Maker.

When this was finished, the tribunal carried the tiny blue corpse through the streets for all to see. They told the milling islanders that the Maker had seen fit to let the child die in peace rather than live in a world where it would be damned. Once the crowd was dispersed, the tribunal was left to decide how to dispose of the small body.

The Indian priest thought it should be cremated, and the ashes placed inside a reliquary in his church. It would be a visual reminder for those contemplating adultery.

But Old Mendoza and Maestra Gabriella disagreed, and said that island custom should be observed. This meant offering the tiny corpse to the sharks, as was always done with stillborn babies. This situation was nearer to that than any they could think of.

The custom of making an offering to the sharks was so that a stillborn child could then be reincarnated as a shark. The corpse was wrapped in colorful shrouds and flowers, then dropped from a boat in open water.

If the sharks accepted the offering, it was considered a sign of benevolence. A fiesta would be held in the plaza. The family of the child accepted by sharks would be immune to shark attacks for the rest of their lives. This protection extended as far as third cousins, but did not include spouses coming into a family after the offering was made and accepted.

Many an island woman prayed for at least one stillborn child sometime in life. Two stillborn children in the same family was considered extremely good fortune. Not only did it protect the other family members from shark attacks. But it also passed that luck to the following generation. Naturally, this all depended on the good faith of the sharks themselves.

The Indian priest stood his ground regarding cremation. A murdered child is not the same as a stillborn one, he said. To offer a murdered child to the sharks would violate their pact with the sea. Besides, he added, sharks were wise enough to discern the smell of infanticide from the pure, embryonic smell of a stillborn child.

Maestra Gabriella and Old Mendoza saw the truth in what the priest said, and they deferred to him in the matter. That afternoon, the corpse of the infant was cremated. The ashes were placed in a reliquary on the church altar.

Down at the conch mountain for the next few mornings, Old Mendoza was astounded how many dreams were told about fire. It seemed to him that everyone had slept in flames.

GARIBALDI NIGHT SONGS

The frail whore in black lace teeters drunkenly in high heels across wet flagstone. Dozens of mariachis gather in groups. The night air swells with songs plucked from catguts. Music weeps louder at night. Ask the darkness, it will tell you.

Young mariachis strut in tight jeans with carefully arranged crotches. They anticipate music and whatever else the night can provide. The old mariachis huddle in round-shouldered circles. Their faces and hands are creased, played out. Bit by bit, songs are escaping them.

Nearby, a dilapidated midway sports dart games. Break a balloon and win trinkets from Japan. Pulque bars at the edge of the plaza are cheek to cheek with people never quite done with forgetting.

But none of this is the main attraction. Remain long enough and you will see the fire-eater. He arrives with his partner, a deaf mute who breaks empty whiskey bottles on the flagstone. Dead drunk, the fire-eater holds a flame to his mouth, misses, and chars his face instead. Just a boy, he smells of old burns when he sings his madman's *Jalisco*.

People scatter as night fades. Yet they know that another night is soon coming, another night that festers with songs and dreams of songs and souls of songs.

More than mariachis depend on this.

ANNA

Not fully awake, Anna looks distantly around the small room in which she makes her living. The stark white stucco walls are a definition of austerity except for the crucifix, bloody and dramatic even by Mexican standards. The cross was hung on the wall by the woman who rents the room to Anna. She has left it there so as not to offend the old woman.

It means nothing to Anna, this cross. She has changed greatly since coming to the island. She has hardened, and she does not wonder why. Maybe she blames it on the coarse sea water. But it is also her spirit which has grown hard.

Each blistering hot night is followed by a violently brazen white dawn. A wave of heat hovers above the island. Anna sways through the days, not counting or comparing them.

Her room is dimly lit and tightly shuttered, in a small house just up from Fly Alley. This is the name of the area across from the small marina, where fishermen bring in their small skiffs. More often than not, those small boats are laden heavily with giant tortugas.

Down near the shore, in Fly Alley, fishermen smash the heads of the tortugas, executing them with short vigorous blows from the skiff anchors. Then they cut up the giant turtles, keeping the best meat and the shells for themselves. What is leftover is thrown into Fly Alley, where the sun begins to devour the rest. What native women do not gather in their skirts is left for the flies.

Swarms of flies gather there, not unlike the heat wave of the white dawn. The flies survey the leftover kill like miniature vultures that circle helpless prey. After hardly any hesitation at all, the flies descend. They remain until every last morsel is consumed, until nothing is left and the blood has dried in the sand.

Anna's room is tightly shuttered, not so much because of the tortuga killings, but because she cannot bear what follows in Fly Alley, the rush of want and greed she knows will come.

Now, ever so early and the air already stifling from the wave of heat, she feels beads of sweat on her neck and her breasts. She does not bother to wipe them away. She knows that more will follow. She yawns, and when she looks around the room this time, it is as if for the first time.

Her eyes come to rest on a white sailor uniform on the floor, in the corner. The uniform is in a heap, abandoned there hastily. Anna looks away from the uniform and runs her hands over her stomach and her breasts. Then, as she lifts her head from the pillow and looks across the bed, she sees him. A man, on his side, asleep and facing her. She wonders what she knows about this man. All she can be sure about is that he has already paid.

She also knows, by rote, that he will soon awaken. He will shift his position and open his eyes. He will leave passiveness behind in his dreams. He will open his eyes and look around the room, collecting his thoughts. Then it will begin again.

She is thirsty, but to get up from bed would awaken the still sleeping sailor. She considers this, then tries to forget her thirst. But before she can complete the thought, the man stirs. His hands reach out and grab her shoulders. The hands pull at her like she is some limp rag doll.

He pulls her across his body. His hands show her the course he wants her to follow. She responds, for what she believes is the thousandth time.

When she closes her eyes, she can still feel the roughness of his hands. She can still smell his sweat and his breath. But all she can see is a swarm of flies.

BECOMING SHAKESPEARE

(After Borges)

It could happen. To you, beneath your roof, some night or afternoon. Suddenly, without warning. But it could just as well never happen. To you. No matter what.

No, it could happen to someone else, the poet who is your best friend. His day, then. His parade. Perhaps.

Probably it will be different. It won't happen to you or your friend. No, the moment might come far away, an aboriginal scrawl, Tiananmen dream, rain forest song. Or from a cave, coaxed into light.

And go unnoticed. Because no one can imagine such a thing so far away, in another tongue and town, for someone other than ourselves.

WANTS

From the window, moon glow showers the room. Inside that room, inside a dream, her hands grasp, dark against brilliant sheets. Her fingers never stop their reaching.

She crawls through the dream toward a distant voice that begs to be touched. A weary voice, alive and calling for a long time. So long, in fact, that she no longer recognizes the voice as her own.

Her cat, on the sill, watches her hands, then looks back out the window. Toward the sky. When the moon comes closer, he will gather it inside his paw.

THE CLOTHESLINE

The kitchen towel, rarely used. The cloth from her art studio, where no work has been accomplished. Sheets from *her* bed, where her husband refused to sleep. *His* blanket, from the bunk in the garage.

The pink dress, in which they almost buried their daughter. The sun is merciless. Drying comes about, quickly. But in the late afternoon, when she comes to take things down, the pink dress resists her touch. Once she loosens the clothes pins, it has its own mind. It rises, into the sky, out of her reach. She runs after it across the yard, down the street, dodging cars. Her eyes, so accustomed to tears, begin again. Waterfalls.

Later, in the parking lot at the shopping mall, she must stop to catch her breath. Hands on her knees, she watches in disbelief. The pink dress ascends, guided by angels.

In seconds it disappears completely.

FOREVER

They form a procession, all those gone, so many now across the years. Once you begin to believe they have vanished entirely, they appear again.

They persist, after time and even memory try to shroud them. They last, in spite of the great sequence that carries everything steadily on.

They startle us on a walk in the woods. Wait for us in clearings where light gives life to old and brittle leaves.

TOWARD A FARMHOUSE

The road, muddled by grass, leads home just as it leads away. Eloquently, through trees, a field. Trees must understand this compulsion we have for going, for roads and why we follow them. The man you see, the denim figure ahead of you, does not know if he understands this much.

His life is some vague prayer of routine, urging his sheep on, finding room in his head for his thoughts, each of them night bound, drifting toward sleep. He considers the day just done and those to come. Of long trudging, the mud of years. The silence of dusk is pierced by bleats. By wind from the north. Trees gather their limbs, then let them fly free.

The wind will last until the farmhouse is gone, until the road, coming or going, is forgotten. When even the man's memory becomes muddled and overgrown, scattered across time.

WINGS

When you hear them, when time draws them to you like moths, try to avoid panic. So many fluttering winged beings, their feathers so soft in final air, they come to spirit you away. To an unknown place.

Here, though, you know everything. Here, there is nothing left to learn. Ever again.

That is not what causes panic. Panic is brother to fear that comes from so many rushing wings at once, descending, gathering around you, lifting you aloft.

Once you rise with them, fear will fall away. Fear is something you will no longer need to know.

ANOTHER PIZZA NIGHT

The fire is burning out of control now. The once grand department store simmers with light and heat. Everything - jewelry, candies, glassware, hosiery, ties, kitchen wares, appliances, furs, items in layaway, even the burly, sleeping security guard - melts into a strange chemical cloud that shrouds display cases, obscures the eerie smiles of mannequins, clogs the aisles, floats up the down escalator and rides the elevators where no operators work the controls.

She watches from across the street, from her apartment window. Sad because she put in forty long years at the store, beginning as a novitiate in gift wrap and ascending to manager of fine bras. But the sadness leaves, like the burning building goes away, when she closes her eyes.

The heat from the fire still intense on her skin, she is adrift on a raft on a Caribbean island, in a hotel pool at high noon. If she squints a bit, allowing the aura of flames to lick at her vision, she is floating on a bed in a cabana, an island man filling her with heat.

It is a problem for her. Always such a faithful store employee, she should rightfully keep a vigil, eyes wide open, and watch the walls of her dear store collapse. But of course this will make the island man disappear, and much too soon as far as she is concerned.

Let it burn, she decides. She pulls the man with dark skin closer to her. She will not open her eyes again. Will not watch the humiliating end of her beloved store. After all, she has been its mistress her entire adult life.

Besides, she is starving. She knows that the pizza delivery man cannot even dream of coming down the street with the store on fire. If she keeps making love to the island man, she will not think of food.

So she keeps her eyes closed, not seeing two hundred firemen down in the street. Fighting the inferno, each of them is wishing he was with the woman he left at home.

She does not see the firemen run as the wall facing the street falls outward, into the apartment house itself. So lost in lovemaking, she is not aware how the fire, in its jealousy, angrily climbs the brick facade of her building. How it scours the windows for the right one, where a once faithful lover has so cruelly looked away. How the chemical cloud, so full of all things, drifts through the white lace curtains of the cabana on its way to a kill.

KINGDOMS

They had lived in the dark, in its midst, some fifteen years. Ever since the children left, fleeing the house of perfection. And, the house of boredom.

He considered all this, driving through the night to their mountain cabin. Oncoming headlights, though there were very few, illuminated the snow on either side of the road. The darkness that followed each passing car triggered his thoughts back to the curving black road. The road seemed to double back, then surge ahead, always elusive. It was treacherous going, as if there might be something evil along that road that night, as if something might, at any second, hiss and spit at them.

She sat beside but away from him. Giddy in the dark, she hummed along with the big band music on the radio and rubbed her thighs. These years she was spent, the same as he. And they both knew it all too well.

Already, on this late night road, they were quite beyond the boredom that had seeped beneath the doors of their marriage. Then, above the sound of the music and the heater, she spoke. Best slow down, she said. He turned up the radio and scanned channels, looking for something she would not like. Best slow down, she repeated, louder than before.

Instead, he pressed his foot on the accelerator, hard. In his mind, he was going to rise above their shell of a family. To him, they would rise up from that twisting, viperlike road. They would glide through the dark sky where stars crisscrossed the blackness. He imagined himself going beyond all this. He didn't know for how long, or even when he would return. He had bourbon singing in his blood.

She sighed, forgetting the song she had been humming. Looking away from him, she saw her sad reflection in the window. She imagined a snake was in their cabin up ahead on that road. It was a snake that waited patiently in the night. She hoped that it was a very poisonous one, and that it was coiled on his side of the bed.

He too was dreaming of a snake. His snake, also patient, had lived in the world long enough to know that waiting counted for much, maybe for everything. His snake was along this very road, this very night. It was coiled on the side of the road where he planned to push her out.

And though they both knew this was the dead of winter and snakes would be hibernating, it didn't matter. They were both drunk, as usual. For them, snakes would come out this night. These snakes could be commanded. These snakes were a necessity.

It happened quickly, both of them silent and lost in thought. In an instant he passed out and his hands loosened from the steering wheel. Panicked, she looked out the window and once again came face to face with her reflection. Her eyes were frozen. When at last she broke her gaze and tried to take the wheel herself, it was too late.

The car seemed to fly, as he had wanted it to do. But it flew to the side, into the air, finally falling hundreds of feet to the snowbound trees below.

Beneath the roots of those trees, snakes huddled in balls, sleeping, awaiting the thaw. They dreamed of possibilities. Of warm beds in mountain cabins, where the people, for one reason or another, had gone away.

And, in their dreams, the people never returned. The sleeping snakes knew how waiting could count for much. How, if they waited long enough, even kingdoms could change hands.

WOMBS

In the beginning, she was a womb, the same as he. This is how they imagined themselves. As promises, possibilities. Upon meeting, they realized they were part of something larger. Alive and growing. Many promises.

But it was not until much later, when they were old and frail, that they understood how they and everyone were enclosed in another, even larger womb. It contained all thoughts, sounds, whatever could be seen, in dreams and not. It even contained everything ever forgotten, by anyone.

On and on. Huge, like an endless room. It enclosed the world. And if they were very quiet, they could almost hear it. Breathing, lasting. Maybe shuffling inside an even larger womb.

THIS BED

Wide enough for the seas. Every phylum of hope. Lava to churn below. Ample reason. Cellar of wisdom. Music, drifting.

Around it, a house with purpose, fire in its hearth. In other rooms, space for the living and the dead. Hallways where they might console each other.

Room for gods, but only the just.

Always a lit path there.

DRUG STORE (1927)

(After Edward Hopper)

Vials of dyed apothecary water beckon, offer deliverance from illnesses real, dreamed, perhaps only imagined. Freedom from so many maladies we cannot know them all, their names, how they come to us. Or where they will leave us when they're done.

Promise me a cure and I'll swear eternal love, even if no such thing still exists. Cures, like loves, are only hopes that come in doses, measured elixirs, glowing potions from a shaman's rite, this storefront dream.

EDWARD HOPPER'S WOMEN

So easy to call them fragile, but that is how they appear, their eyes fixed on something still unnamed. Moving and not. Inside the wide world of a room. Or through a window, staring into the void.

In the end, all that truly matters is that they continue to gaze. That their eyes have not yet closed in private defeat, even if the world itself has given up the cause. Their faith is not in what they see, but in what they seek.

Out there, beyond a world always so very close to breaking.

WOMAN IN STONE

She never knew his name. That for so long she was only a sketch in his head. She listened as he worked, could almost hear his world. Imagined she could almost know him. His tools in combat with stone. She stood in the hard darkness, imagining sun.

One day, he went away. She was abandoned, in between worlds, one foot stepping free from the limestone block.

He was ill. When he finally returned, his work was riddled with urgency. She could feel the chisel's haste. The man was dying, but she could not understand the concept. All she could think about was sun. For so long it had been but a sketch in her head.

When he was finished, he looked like an old man. When he lay down to rest, he never woke up again. Maybe, she thought, he no longer needed sun.

She was different. She would never be without it. Bathed in the golden shafts of morning, she no longer had to imagine.

UNDER A RIVERBED SKY

In the evening, we come looking for them. Words. Our city, its dazzling glow, miles behind us now. Hope, the ancient parasite, sits on our shoulders in a carrion dream. But how else can we go about it, our work?

A dark blue land beckons us. Here, we learn not how a night sky shrouds a field, but how a moon can coax it out. All around us, things alive. Leaves, stalks, wild berries, animals of night. All come from the shadows to be counted, to meet the wide flat hand of the sky.

If you are patient, moonlight will find them for you. Words. They glimmer in the dirt like treasure buried in haste. Easily touched, had. Others hide deeper, their lights extinguished.

Sadly, some are lost for good. Pressed down deep into earth. Waiting for another time. A different moon. Forgotten, abandoned like an old Celtic dream.

TREES

You have never ceased your reaching out, not in all of time or dance of seasons. Or, even in the time we have somehow recoiled from you.

Where have we gone? Somewhere, anywhere, nowhere. Into the air. Not into silence, though. No, caught inside a speeding pace that frazzles, that wearies in its dizzying wake. Because of this, time shrouds your presence. I pass without seeing you, knowing you. Even to remember how long you reigned before my own kind.

For us, it is never enough to merely be. Stand, stretch, eventually fall. Envy of time is why. We clutch at it dutifully, hoping to become an honored member of its court.

How long did it take you to realize how time passes without seeing, not even to acknowledge your presence?

And did it feel like this?

BAREFOOT

When the late movie ended, we turned on the light. Next to us on the bed, the dog was sleeping. Time to time, her feet twitched. She was running this way and that in a dream.

You pointed to the dog's feet, those dark pads on the underside. They were rough and crusty and aged. Travelers. They told the tale.

When the dog was young, you said, those pads were smooth and black. Even shiny. That's what the world does, we decided.

Which led us to our own feet. We had an investigation. It was a similar tale, of course, what the world does to you if you go out to meet it. Our feet were stories in themselves. Wrinkled and tough-skinned. Maps.

Which reminded me what I'd heard about the dead. How they are buried barefoot in their coffins. How they go feet first into eternity.

No matter if it's hot there. Or even if they must walk on ice. And how the walk itself never ends.

THE NIGHT BATTLES

Armies are coming. Not seen, but heard from out there, beyond the river and fields. Beyond every small hill rising inside a mind set for sleep.

In that hazy place where dreams root and germinate, the moon abandons the sky. It plunges into the underground of long remembering.

It is then that the armies come. Phantom generals shout orders that ricochet in our latex world. I wait to see the glimmer of swords through trees dyed by night.

Asleep, facing away, you see none of this. Armies coming and going, the dead borne away. Their movements are metaphors for my own indecision.

Do I go with them or remain here? Do I refuse to decide? Insomnia's banner waves on the dark, digital field, in the air-conditioned night.

Tonight, I will not decide. This night, every battle will be fought inside.

DOGS, DREAMING

Late at night, my house or yours, dreaming is best in a warm dry room. Better still if outside darkness howls, if wind fans fires of sleep.

Their dreams must be memories. Old hunts, saliva and instinct. Pressed tight in a lurching pack. Watching a dawn grey sky. Waiting for the waterfowl bounty.

Or, perhaps they dream of being human, inside a warm house on a wild night. Sitting back, watching the dogs dream.

My house or yours, a fear persists that someone somewhere will wake, make the house and the dreams and everything inside them disappear.

WHY THE DARKNESS PRAYS

There is a sound I hear some nights, in my house, or in the streets if I cannot sleep and instead decide to go walking. In the sand streets on this island, my steps make no sound. The small noise of my breath is the only thing to give my presence away. But I feel no one can hear me.

If they are awake, they are wishing they were asleep. They are listening for, counting in fact, their own breaths. If they are asleep, they are gripped inside the hands of dreams. They are too busy to hear someone walking by, outside their houses or their dreams.

It is a particular sound I hear some nights. Not snores drifting from windows in houses. Or wind ruffling the palm trees. Not even the sound of water breaking at the shore. No, the sound I hear is the voice of night. The very language of the darkness itself. A low, musical voice that stirs in the shadows.

It is, I know, the darkness praying. And hoping, no doubt, that things might change.

The darkness prays that it might rise up and out of itself. Somehow. That it might leave the eternal cage of night and live, if only for a short time, in the light. That it will not always be this way, condemned to the only fate it has ever known.

But of course this cannot change, this fact of the darkness, no matter how lonely. After all, any prayer of supplication only carries so far. It is such a very long way to heaven. A prayer cannot be heard everywhere at once. At the shoreline, whispered from palm fronds, sliding so sadly off the roofs of simple huts. Even this prayer, uttered by the night itself, won't change a thing.

But here and there, the prayer makes a sound, straining to be heard. I come across it in shadows and sometimes in moonlight. A small and weary song, tired of being sung. The prayer is audible because it sounds like nothing else in the world. And because it is so unbearably desperate.

I cannot sleep with the sound of such desperation. Instead, I walk the sand streets, and hope to comfort the darkness. Somehow. Tell it that it is not alone most nights.